dusk to dawn
and
midday thoughts

dusk to dawn
and
midday thoughts

A Collection of Poems by Sydney Guerrette

WALNUT STREET
— PUBLISHING —

ISBN 978-1-7342750-5-6

Walnut Street Publishing
1645 S Holtzclaw Ave
Chattanooga, TN 37404

to my mom,

*whose light
gave me the confidence
to step out on my own*

*and whose hope
gives me the courage
to move forward with
an open heart and mind*

I AM

Don't compare me to a flower
For all they bring forth is their beauty

Don't compare me to autumn leaves
For they are easily blown by the wind

Don't compare me to a seashell
For the tide persuades them

Don't compare me to a bee
Who only listens to its Majesty

I am of likeness to the earth
Yes scattered, but grounded, firm and BEHOLD,

I am of likeness to the deepest roots,
Protective of growth
Bringing nourishment and life

I am of likeness to the waves,
I shift the culture around me

And I am of likeness to the wind,
Full of soul and SAY

I AM the wonder I crave

What Holds Me Back?

In all sounds, I feel your voice
It aches me

A downward spiral of what is
Soon to be once was
Never to be something good to come

Nothing in balance
In fact
It's all out of balance

I'm not meant to feel balanced
It isn't real
Nothing's real

Why does it occupy so many peoples' thoughts?

Life,
Full of misleading falsehoods

So,
I still ache

Every regret, moment
Lost, gone to waste

I think about them too often
These shadows

Shadows

A proper name for these wretched things
Feelings, thoughts, holding onto you

What happens if you hold too tight to them?

There will be nothing left of you

Will It Ever End?

Perfection lives on borrowed time
Except, it's never borrowed

Only stolen

I should be more furious
But,

I'm not

I live with the body aches

Live with the concerns and anxiety
Even though I'll be sent to an early grave

I've never lacked resilience,
It's something everyone can possess

> But, I've learned the more we retreat,
> The easier it is to
> > *suppress*

That flame
Spark

The glow that fuels your soul

    Perfectionism can
                     snuff   it   *out*

Don't let that get to you now

A Heart's Messy

The more I don't know,
The mɛssiɛr I write

Is it this way for everyone?

Or are there humans
Who are more careful
With their words?

It's all lost on me

I'm not clumsy
Just curious

But my writing reflects my heart
So, if the words are messy

My heart is too

I'm not ashamed of m y s e l f

that's a lie

I'm working to get T H E R E

where I make an effort

To love all I am
Without changing the writing

7

Alone

Am I afraid of being alone?
No, I don't think so

I'm not alone in family
I'm not alone in friends

Why does this question always
f
  a
   l
   l

    down to romantic relations?

You can be or *feel* alone in many ways

Yet, that phrase
I feel most in the air

For the time being,

I feel as if I'm missing out
Or
Undesirable
        w
         h
          a
           t
            e
             v
              e
               r

                t
                 h
                  a
                   t

                    m
                     e
                      a
                       n
                        s

But, I'm also content
And that's okay

I Like Being Different

I like being the only one who's _____

At least, the only one I know of...

But, with this mindset
I lost myself

I set myself apart
Spread myself *too thin*

No grace
No room for error

I form a calloused heart

Turn to *"no one will understand"*s

It's hard to keep friends like this

So, I keep to myself
I don't reach out

I keep to myself
Someone I should be able to rely on

But, I never know with *her*

I never know with *me*

I Choose

Thanks for
keeping me
awake.

Unruly

There's a chaos within
Untamed and
Persuasive

Come too close
And it can *pu l l yo u i n*

On a ledge,
I stand

My arms *s p r e a d* like wings
I feel the air rush towards me

                          This freedom is
liberating
And for once,
                 I finally feel *F R E E*

This chaos inside salutes the wind
They're one in the same

They force whatever's around them
To dance during their reign

Both mother nature's children
Disobedient and
Unruly

One *within* me
One *surrounding* me

I'm closer to life
And *death*
Than I ever realized

The Night Never Lasts

To quiet
To be still

To find warmth in a smile

Little things like gestures, *kind*
Matter.

When I look to the sky
I see not whole **darkness**
But *light* shining through

Is this what hope's like?

Is this what a *quiet*
                    still
                            warmth
Feels like?

To believe there's something
Better, for all of us,
On the other side of the universe

I *choose* to *hope* so.

There's a beauty in the ***darkness***
A beauty in the disarray

But, it can't be as beautiful as
The light piercing through a darkened sky

Can it?

You Go First

Unrevealed thoughts
Sealed
With no postal address

Instead
Set aside
Locked in a *h i d d e n* drawer

Upper left corner of
Your brain

Your heart just
Forgot about them

So, she lets the brain
Deal with it

In order to move forward
Someone
Something
Has to let go

So
One of them
Lets go

16

Time

A beast without *t e e t h*
One of the monstrous halves of our world

Yet, full of wonder

Can something so mysterious
And *finite*
Be so beautiful?

17

Where True Beauty Lies

The majesty of a flower
What we always see
We praise the tiniest of petals
Worship the *even smaller* leaves

But, what about the weeds?
They're seen as unruly creatures
Disturbed
Disturbing to the most *distressed* garden

I tell you
The weeds' roots
Grow deeper than the flowers'

These earthly creatures have more
Of a backbone than the most beautiful
Chrysanthemum

Genuine beauty lies u
               n
                d
                  e
                    r
                      g
                    r
                      o
                        u
                        n
                          d

Deep within soil
Deep within an earthly soul

All of Me

I come with another unique set of prayers
In my own unique frustration
I'm found in my arrogance
Who am I to make requests?

I am the wretched soul
Who pursues the blade
Rather than leave it in its sheath

I've never felt *godly*
Free will isn't a gift,   but
A *curse*
To those who
bend towards
indecisiveness

Who are
Bound
To anxiousness

I can't allow
You to see
Me like this

All my worst parts,   a *deliberate* enemy
So, I stay in my own   *company*

I mustn't allow
You to see
Me like this

I've hollowed certain parts of myself
The worst memories
My *dark* intertwines with my *light*

You can't have
Me or truly know
Me unless
You accept *both*

I am not myself without *both*

You ask, "*Who* will you allow to take up most space?"

We Dream of Other Worlds

In these *dreams*,
We take refuge
In these *worlds*,
We find peace

As I snake into bed,
With lights out
And no one else awake,
All I hear are whispers
They're beckoning me to sleep

Summoning memories
Reconstructing them
So they can play *make-believe*
The subconscious of my imagination
Where there's no limit to *possibility*

I hope my head remembers
Its promise to
My heart

To keep you in the corner
of my darkest memory
For if your vision awakes
My peace will become chaos

My dream
To a nightmare

The only time
I can be still
I'll toss and turn

My bed no longer
A safe place

So, I don't fall asleep
No, I won't fall asleep

There will be no calm
At least until I no longer
Believe you to be a *threat*   *(to me)*

A Weight

In the midst of my grief
It's as if I float on water,   but then

Watch as it slowly
Swallows my body whole

I collapse into *nothing*
My soul becoming *dismal*

Once hollow
Now full of sorrow and   malice

As water fills my lungs
My breath becomes less a nd l e s s

Available

The weight of pain
Surrounds me

But, I will be okay
I will be okay.

This won't last forever
The pain won't last forever
I won't last forever

Just Accept It

In your solitude, I find rest
In your peace, I learn to sleep

The night,
No longer darkness
But, a glimpse of hope

A reminder that what has been
Will lead to what will be

Grace is a funny thing
It's when we are undeserving that
This is gifted to us

If it's a gift
then why do I feel shame?

Why do I let these feelings
Clasp themselves to me?

Like if they let go
They'll disappear
Vanish into t h i n a i r

What would it look like if they did?

What if I accepted this gift?
And found the solitude,
Peace

Just accept it.

Will You Give It the Chance?

Can a heart be lost?
Intentionally.

Sometimes
Your mind has a part
To play

You see
They don't always get
Along

Your heart is
Full of hope

Your mind leads
A cautionary tale

Hope and caution
Have a difficult time
Coexisting

You can be cautious
And hopeful at the same time

But, be careful
To sway more in
One direction than
The other

Too much caution
Borderlines fear

And fear will lock
Your heart up
Whenever you give it
The chance

My Turn

They've clipped my wings
What will I do?

They've clipped my wings
Will this hold me back from my truth?

They've clipped my wings
This won't keep me in one place for long

They've clipped *my wings*
So wingless, I *must* learn to be free

To the Women in My Life

Thank you for showing me what
Love is.

Wearing your hearts
On your sleeves,
The *invaluable* strength
Found in the midst of hardship

Your *resilience*,
A badge of *honor*

Having been through so much,
You've made it to where
You are now

Here.

Breathing.

Full of life.

Despite all that's been said
And done to you
Your head is held *high*

Moving forward,
Your *kindness* never lost
Its way, love

Flight

Let me show you
A world with no limits

A world full of
Connection

A world where the dreamers
Rule

Take into consideration
The way you feel as soon
As you let go of
Others' expectations

It feels as though a
Burden is lifted

Pen to paper,
Paper to Instrument,
Instrument to Stage,

Limitlessness
Swoops around me

Keeps me on
My toes

Wingless,
Yet,

I take *flight*

www.ingramcontent.com/pod-product-compliance
Lightning Source LLC
Chambersburg PA
CBHW011232120626
46549CB00008B/3246